Christmas Piano Sol

For All Piano Methods

Table of Contents

Christmas Piano Solos Level 3 is designed for use with the third book of any piano method.

Concepts in *Christmas Piano Solos Level 3*:

Range

Symbols

pp, p, mp, mf, f, ff, ♯, ♭, ♮, *ritard, a tempo, 8va, loco*

simple pedaling

Rhythm

4/4 time signature
3/4 time signature
¢ cut time
swing eighths

Intervals

2nd, 3rd, 4th, 5th, 6th
melodic and harmonic

Three-note Chords

ISBN 978-0-7935-8579-3

Hal • Leonard®

Visit Hal Leonard Online at
www.halleonard.com

Contact us:
Hal Leonard
7777 West Bluemound Road
Milwaukee, WI 53213
Email: info@halleonard.com

In Europe, contact:
Hal Leonard Europe Limited
42 Wigmore Street
Marylebone, London, W1U 2RN
Email: info@halleonardeurope.com

In Australia, contact:
Hal Leonard Australia PTY. Ltd.
4 Lentara Court
Cheltenham, Victoria, 3192 Australia
Email: info@halleonard.com.au

We Wish You A Merry Christmas

With spirit

Traditional English Folksong

Accompaniment (Student plays one octave higher than written.)

With spirit

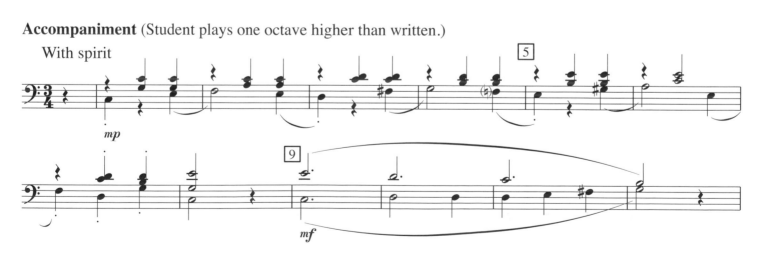

tid - ings   for   Christ - mas   and   a   Hap - py   New   Year.   We

mp

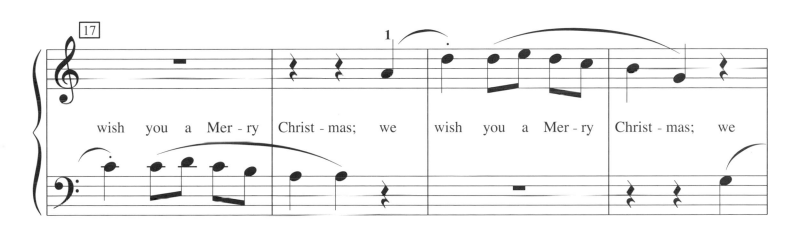

wish   you   a   Mer - ry   Christ - mas;   we   wish   you   a   Mer - ry   Christ - mas;   we

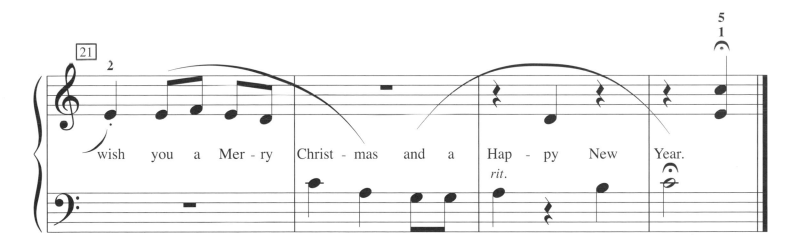

wish   you   a   Mer - ry   Christ - mas   and   a   Hap - py   New   Year.

rit.

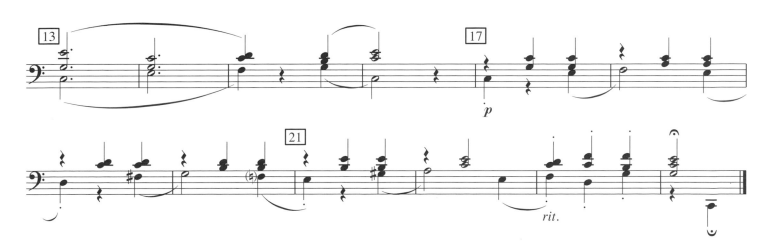

p

rit.

3

The First Noel

Moderately, with expression

17th Century English Carol

The __ first __ No - el the __ an - gel did say was to

cer - tain poor shep - herds in fields as they lay; in __

fields __ where __ they lay __ keep - ing their sheep, on a

Accompaniment (Student plays one octave higher than written.)

Moderately, with expression

With pedal *mp*

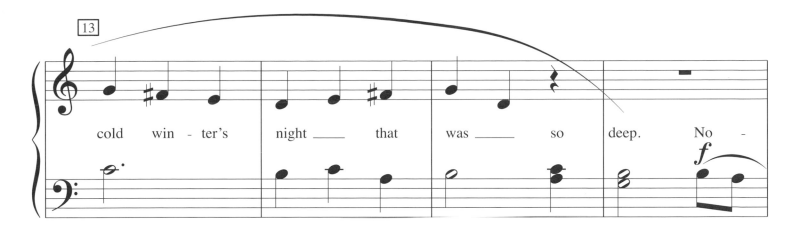

cold win - ter's night _____ that was _____ so deep. No -

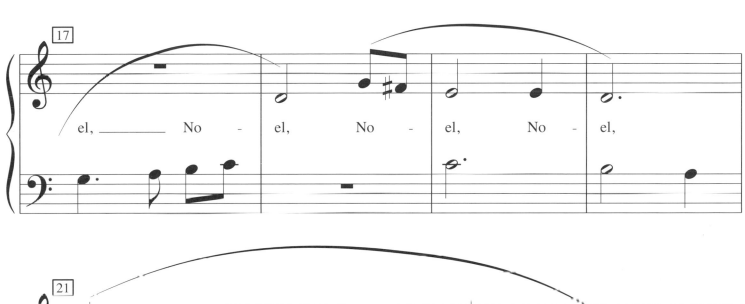

el, _____ No - el, No - el, No - el,

born is the King _____ of Is - ra - el.

rit.

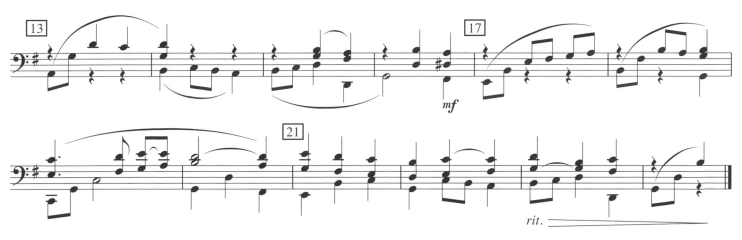

My Favorite Things
from THE SOUND OF MUSIC

Lyrics by Oscar Hammerstein II
Music by Richard Rodgers

Accompaniment (Student plays one octave higher than written.)

Rudolph The Red-Nosed Reindeer

Music and Lyrics by
Johnny Marks

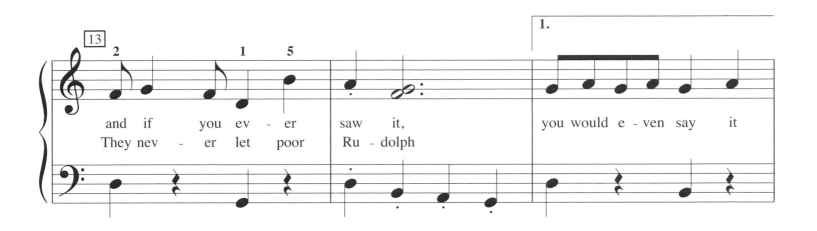

and if you ev - er saw it,
They nev - er let poor Ru - dolph

you would e - ven say it

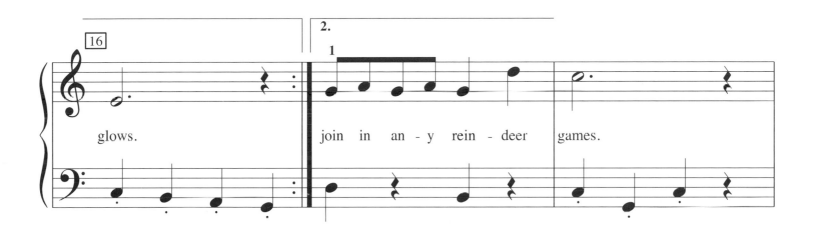

glows.

join in an - y rein - deer games.

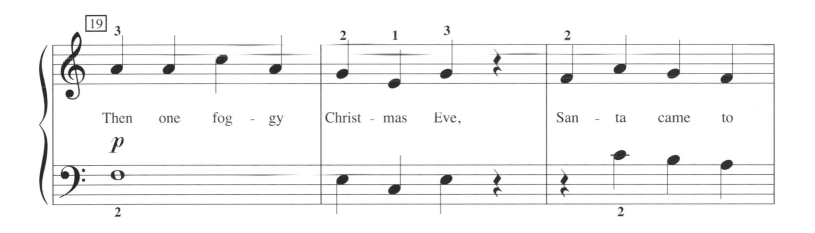

Then one fog - gy Christ - mas Eve,

San - ta came to

p

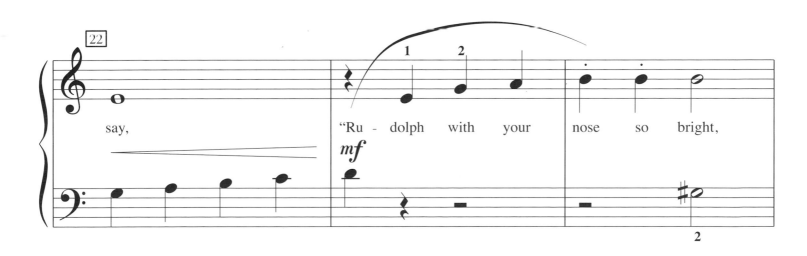

say,

"Ru - dolph with your nose so bright,

mf

9

won't you guide my sleigh to-night?"— Then all the rein-deer

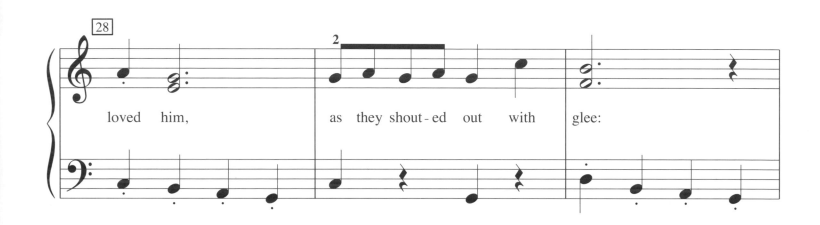

loved him, as they shout-ed out with glee:

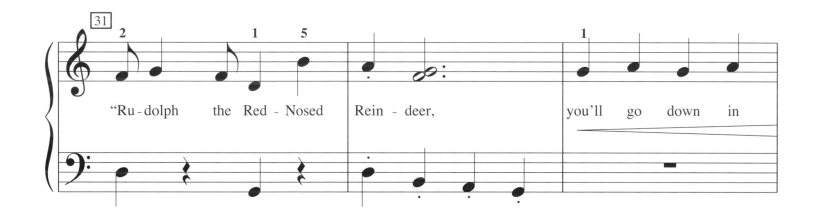

"Ru-dolph the Red - Nosed Rein - deer, you'll go down in

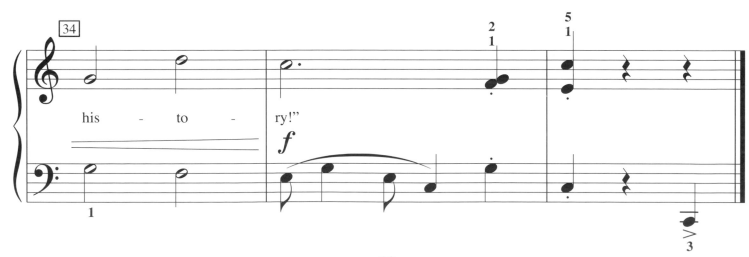

his - to - ry!"

O Christmas Tree

Delicately

Traditional German Carol

The Chipmunk Song

Words and Music by
Ross Bagdasarian

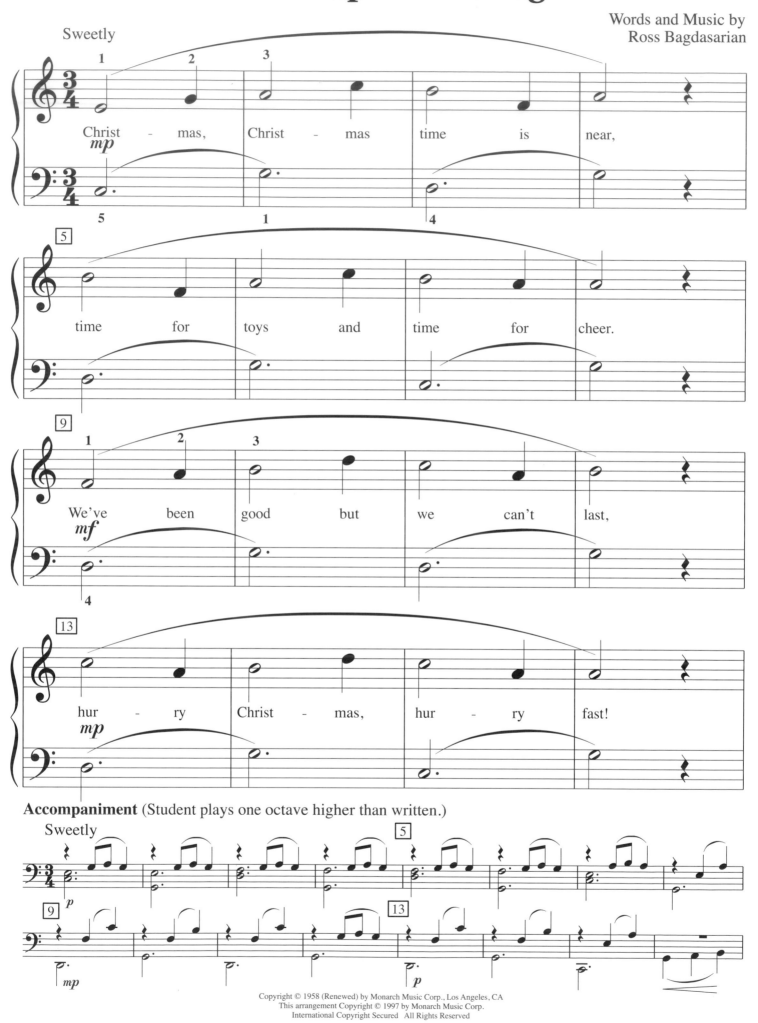

Accompaniment (Student plays one octave higher than written.)

Carol Of The Bells

Bright tempo

Traditional Ukrainian Carol

Frosty The Snow Man

Words and Music by Steve Nelson
and Jack Rollins

Fros - ty the Snow Man was a jol - ly hap - py soul, with a
Fros - ty the Snow Man knew the sun was hot that day, so he

corn cob pipe and a but - ton nose and two eyes made out of coal.
said, "Let's run and we'll have some fun now be - fore I melt a - way."

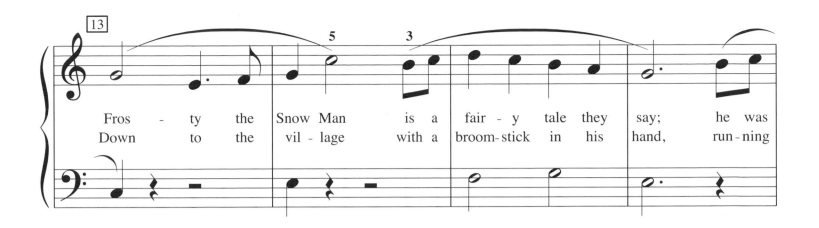

Fros - ty the Snow Man is a fair - y tale they say; he was
Down to the vil - lage with a broom-stick in his hand, run - ning

made of snow but the chil - dren know how he came to life one day. There
here and there all a - round the square say-ing, "Catch me if you can." He

must have been some mag - ic in that old silk hat they found, for
led them down the streets of town right to the traf - fic cop, and he

when they placed it on his head he be - gan to dance a - round. Oh,
on - ly paused a mo - ment when he heard him hol - ler, "Stop!" For

Fros - ty, the Snow Man was a - live as he could be, and the
Fros - ty, the Snow Man had to hur - ry on his way, but he

chil - dren say he could laugh and play just the same as you and me.
waved good - bye say - in', "Don't you cry; I'll be back a - gain some - day."

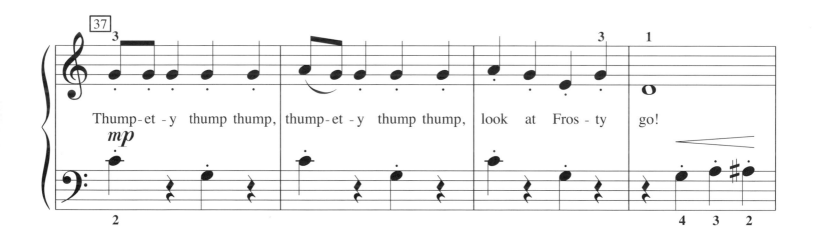

Thump - et - y thump thump, thump - et - y thump thump, look at Fros - ty go!

mp

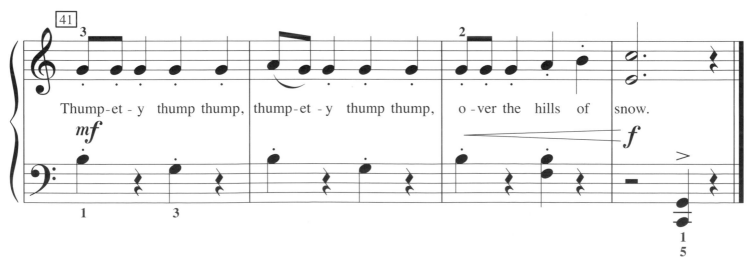

Thump - et - y thump thump, thump - et - y thump thump, o - ver the hills of snow.

mf   *f*

Deck The Hall

Joyfully

Traditional Welsh Carol

We Need A Little Christmas

from MAME

Music and Lyric by
Jerry Herman

Rockin' Around The Christmas Tree

Music and Lyrics by
Johnny Marks

With a bounce (Swing eighths)

Rock-in' a - round the Christ-mas tree at the Christ-mas par - ty hop;
Rock-in' a - round the Christ-mas tree; let the Christ-mas spir - it ring.

mis-tle-toe hung where you can see ev - 'ry cou - ple tries to stop.
Lat - er we'll have some pump-kin pie and we'll

do some ca - rol - ing. You will get a sen - ti - men - tal feel-ing when you

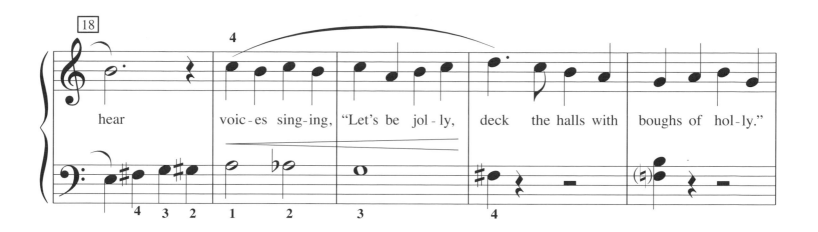

hear   voic-es sing-ing, "Let's be jol-ly,   deck   the halls with   boughs of hol-ly."

Rock-in' a-round the   Christ-mas tree; have a   hap-py hol-i-day.

mf

Ev-'ry-one danc-ing   mer-ri-ly   in the   new   old   fash-ioned

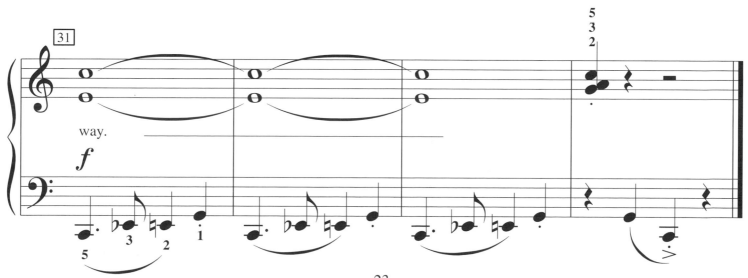

way.

f

Hal Leonard Student Piano Library

The Hal Leonard Student Piano Library has great music and solid pedagogy delivered in a truly creative and comprehensive method. It's that simple. A creative approach to learning using solid pedagogy and the best music produces skilled musicians! Great music means motivated students, inspired teachers and delighted parents. It's a method that encourages practice, progress, confidence, and best of all – success.

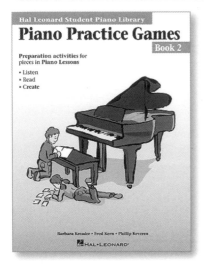

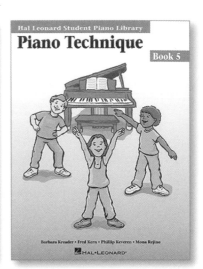

PIANO LESSONS BOOK 1
00296177 Book/Online Audio............................ $9.99
00296001 Book Only $7.99

PIANO PRACTICE GAMES BOOK 1
00296002 .... $7.99

PIANO SOLOS BOOK 1
00296568 Book/Online Audio............................ $9.99
00296003 Book Only $7.99

PIANO THEORY WORKBOOK BOOK 1
00296023 .... $7.50

PIANO TECHNIQUE BOOK 1
00296563 Book/Online Audio............................ $8.99
00296105 Book Only $7.99

NOTESPELLER FOR PIANO BOOK 1
00296088 .... $7.99

TEACHER'S GUIDE BOOK 1
00296048 .... $7.99

PIANO LESSONS BOOK 2
00296178 Book/Online Audio............................ $9.99
00296006 Book Only $7.99

PIANO PRACTICE GAMES BOOK 2
00296007 .... $8.99

PIANO SOLOS BOOK 2
00296569 Book/Online Audio............................ $8.99
00296008 Book Only $7.99

PIANO THEORY WORKBOOK BOOK 2
00296024 .... $7.99

PIANO TECHNIQUE BOOK 2
00296564 Book/Online Audio............................ $8.99
00296106 Book Only $7.99

NOTESPELLER FOR PIANO BOOK 2
00296089 .... $6.99

PIANO LESSONS BOOK 3
00296179 Book/Online Audio............................ $9.99
00296011 Book Only $7.99

PIANO PRACTICE GAMES BOOK 3
00296012 .... $7.99

PIANO SOLOS BOOK 3
00296570 Book/Online Audio............................ $8.99
00296013 Book Only $7.99

PIANO THEORY WORKBOOK BOOK 3
00296025 .... $7.99

PIANO TECHNIQUE BOOK 3
00296565 Book/Enhanced CD Pack $8.99
00296114 Book Only $7.99

NOTESPELLER FOR PIANO BOOK 3
00296167 .... $7.99

PIANO LESSONS BOOK 4
00296180 Book/Online Audio............................ $9.99
00296026 Book Only $7.99

PIANO PRACTICE GAMES BOOK 4
00296027 .... $6.99

PIANO SOLOS BOOK 4
00296571 Book/Online Audio............................ $8.99
00296028 Book Only $7.99

PIANO THEORY WORKBOOK BOOK 4
00296038 .... $7.99

PIANO TECHNIQUE BOOK 4
00296566 Book/Online Audio............................ $8.99
00296115 Book Only $7.99

PIANO LESSONS BOOK 5
00296181 Book/Online Audio............................ $9.99
00296041 Book Only $8.99

PIANO SOLOS BOOK 5
00296572 Book/Online Audio............................ $9.99
00296043 Book Only $7.99

PIANO THEORY WORKBOOK BOOK 5
00296042 .... $8.99

PIANO TECHNIQUE BOOK 5
00296567 Book/Online Audio............................ $8.99
00296116 Book Only $8.99

ALL-IN-ONE PIANO LESSONS
00296761 Book A – Book/Online Audio $10.99
00296776 Book B – Book/Online Audio $10.99
00296851 Book C – Book/Online Audio $10.99
00296852 Book D – Book/Online Audio $10.99

Prices, contents, and availability subject to change without notice.

HAL•LEONARD®
www.halleonard.com